SIX WORD LESSONS ON

HR Practices for A Productive Workforce

100 Lessons to Bring Your Workforce Together

Juli Bacon

Published by Pacelli Publishing
Bellevue, Washington

CONTRIBUTORS

JB Consulting Systems team:

Suzanne Meyers-Hubner

Rebecca House

Apryl Ackley

Kristin Johnson

Robin Johnson

JBConsultingSystems.com

Six-Word Lessons on HR Practices for a Productive Workforce

Cover and interior designed by Pacelli Publishing
Cover photo by iStock
Author photo: *Photography by Carol Hook*

Copyright © 2019 by Juli Bacon

Published by Pacelli Publishing
9905 Lake Washington Blvd. NE, #D-103
Bellevue, Washington 98004
PacelliPublishing.com

ISBN 10: 1-933750-72-3
ISBN-13: 978-1-933750-72-9

Dedication

To my incredible, dedicated team at JB Consulting Systems. You are the fabric of the company.

To my children, James and Jessica, who have inspired me to be the best person I can be.

Contents

Introduction

How do you learn Human Resources? Good question. I can honestly say that even for as long as I have been in Human Resources, I am still learning. There are so many facets and nuances to the field of Human Resources, and how you approach one topic or one particular issue can change with new laws and new generations. It is a lifelong study in people for me.

Rather than trying to write volumes, and that is what it would take, I loved the concept of six-word lessons. Providing you with bite-sized tips in several common areas for Human Resources appealed to me. My company approaches Human Resources from my philosophy that your company is as good as your employees, so take care of them. Happy employees lead to happy clients, which lead to happy owners. Learn what inspires and motivates your employees, hire well and get out of the way and let them do their job. It was a pleasure working on this book with several members of the JB Consulting Systems team. This book would not have been written without their contributions. From planning to writing to editing, my team pushed this along and made it better than I could have done on my own. I hope you find something useful to help you as a manager, owner or employee.

Begin the Race, Recruit to Win

1

The pitfalls of writing job descriptions

The job description should be a description of what the job is; not how to do the job. Don't miss important components, such as ADA-compliant language like key essential job functions and physical requirements. A strong job description also includes a clear summary, specific essential functions and qualifications needed to perform the job.

2

How to write an effective ad

Strike hard and strike fast when writing your job ad. Most job seekers today begin their search for a new position while on their mobile devices, utilizing search engines and skimming quickly through job listings before moving on. Creative posts will gain their interest and keep it. Catch their attention with cleverly crafted words and key information to draw them to your job within the first sentence.

3

Listing and advertising your open position

To generate interest in a position you need to cast a wide enough net to attract the right candidates. Utilize the most advantageous internet job sites (they change often), including industry-specific and professional organizations. Consider posting on your social media pages, personal and professional, as well as posting on your website. Be proactive in the search and think outside the box to increase your candidate pool.

Advance prep keeps you on course.

Prepare for the interview process before scheduling candidates, using the job ad and description to determine questions to ask. Maintain legal compliance by asking the same questions of each interviewee. If using an interview team, assign key focus areas to each member to avoid duplication of questions. Retain all documentation used throughout the process, including resumes, applications, interview notes, reference checking, etc., in a hiring file.

5

Realistic expectations around timing and pool

Do your research. It takes time to find the right candidate. The first applicants may not always be the most qualified. Spend the time upfront, avoiding a quick hire that may not be the right fit. Be sure to keep the posting active for a minimum of ten days or more, allowing for full exposure. Consider internal applicants who may have the talent and interest, and may only require some additional training.

6

Use technology to seize the moment.

Stay on top of the various forms of technology to help in the search process. Skype, Facebook, LinkedIn, Zoom and Uber Conference are platforms that will save you money through their free services, and new tools are added daily. Advertising for positions across social media platforms has also become a natural extension of the old tried-and-true methods. Also, rely on current employee referrals to assist in the search.

7

Where to find the top talent

Top talent doesn't always come searching for you. Be open to asking for referrals from friends, employees, your professional network and even recruitment firms. Be prepared to invest time, and also take note of the best times to look for candidates. Studies indicate job seekers search most often at the beginning of the week and mid-mornings. Posting new ads according to those schedules may get you the most value for your ad expenses.

Interviewing is like a first date.

The first impression is a lasting impression. Ensure the candidate feels welcomed. From the initial greeting, sell the company, beginning with introductions, handshakes and the courtesy of offering water to the candidate. Make the candidate relaxed and comfortable, so you can seek out a fit. An interview is a two-way conversation, not an interrogation. Discuss the company and benefits, while you uncover the candidate's skills.

9

Interview the candidate; don't interrogate them.

Both sides of the interview table can be nerve-wracking. Your job as interviewer is to get the best responses to make the right hiring decision. Intimidation tactics or trick questions won't get you the desired result and will often turn good candidates away. Focus your interview on asking good questions aimed at gaining an insightful picture of the candidate.

10

Don't try to steal the show.

Interviewers often talk too much in an interview. The interview is not about you or filling silence. It is about the candidate and determining their fit for the company. Ask questions and listen. Behavioral-based questions draw out how their experience and knowledge could be utilized in the job. A conversation is a natural outcome, but don't let it derail you from the purpose of the interview.

11

Avoid making a bad hiring decision.

Studies show the cost associated with a bad hire can cost an employer $7,000 to $10,000, depending on the position level. Providing an accurate picture of the job and setting clear expectations along the way protects your hiring investment. Be thorough during interviews to ensure you make the right offer to the right candidate. Don't rush or settle in order to fill a position.

12

Keep candidates interested; don't over interview.

When looking to fill a position, be respectful of the candidate's time as well as your own. Avoid unnecessary rounds of interviews and making candidates take multiple trips unless they are essential. Decide on your interview criteria, interview team, rating or comparison techniques, and be ready to make a decision quickly. Candidates will lose interest or accept another job if you don't move swiftly.

13

You can't make the slipper fit.

Finding the right hire boils down to fit and skills necessary to do the job. You might really "like" a candidate's personality, but that doesn't equate to their ability to do the job. Create a criteria checklist or rating system before you begin the interview process to help you compare candidates and weed out those who don't have the skills. This will narrow your pool and make it easier to hire the right candidate.

14

How to prepare an effective offer

Before making an offer, determine your limits--what concessions you're willing to make--if the candidate negotiates. This will speed the negotiation process and ensure a professional approach. In the offer letter, include position title, immediate supervisor, start date and wage, exempt or non-exempt status, benefits eligibility date, and any pre-employment requirements, including drug testing, if applicable.

15

Incorporate personality profiles into the process.

Personality profiles may be fine to use for comparing candidates. However, they should not be the final decision-maker when selecting the right candidate. You must avoid discriminatory systems, and potentially illegal or biased testing. Not everyone tests well, but they can still be a great candidate. Review Equal Employment Opportunity Commission guidelines around testing and ensure that all tests are related to your particular job.

16

Reference checking is a basic necessity.

Skipping the reference check on a potential candidate is a bad idea. Employment references can give you valuable insight into the candidate's past performance in a job, how they approach problems and issues, and other factors that may indicate whether the candidate can do the job. The references can also ensure transparency about their education, previous job roles and dates of employment.

17

Don't stress out over negotiating details.

When you're ready to make an offer, you should have already done your homework regarding the applicant's salary and benefit expectations. Review your compensation guidelines before you strike up the offer discussion. If you lead with a salary too far off the mark, it can quickly derail any further discussion or create long-term internal inequities. Leave room for negotiation, as the candidate may have specific needs of their own.

18

Give a little, get a lot.

Be open and realistic with what you offer a new employee. You may need to be flexible in meeting new employee needs. Benefits come in various shapes and sizes, including non-traditional start/end times, alternative work schedules, reduced pay for additional Paid Time Off, tele-commuting options and more. Be willing to compromise to gain great new talent. Flexibility can be a win/win.

Successful Onboarding Plans Boost Employee Retention

19

One chance at a first impression

Make your new employee feel important and welcomed on their first day. This starts with being prepared and organized before they arrive. Block out time on your calendar to meet with them personally. Communicate with the team and schedule a proper orientation/tour, spending time throughout the day to answer their questions. If others are involved in the orientation, ensure a schedule is prepared and the employee is offered assistance.

Make their first day a success.

Make arrangements before the employee's first day for a desk or work area to be set up for their arrival, including a tested computer and phone, business cards, office supplies, keys/access badge and other items. Assign a team member to help guide and mentor them. Create and use an onboarding checklist for both you and the employee as a reference in the days and weeks to come.

21

Notify others of the new employee.

Introducing the new employee takes very little time, but will be a benefit to all. Send out an introductory email before the employee starts, providing some basic information, such as their name, start date, role, supervisor and a little bit about them. Feel free to ask the new employee for their own bio. Ensure their key contacts within other departments are notified.

22

Establishing and coordinating an effective schedule

Provide the employee with a sense of security and direction with a pre-planned first week schedule. This may include meetings, tours, client visits, training, etc. Ensure that everyone is notified in advance and is given proper expectations on what topics to cover. There is nothing worse than a new employee sitting down with another employee who has no idea what they are supposed to cover.

23

Figuring out the best communication methods

Managers should schedule regular check-ins with their new employee in the form of one-on-one meetings to ensure there are no roadblocks or obstacles out of the gate. This can be daily at first, then weekly, then progress to monthly. The purpose is to communicate openly and often to ensure that expectations are clearly understood, there are no misunderstandings, guidelines are set and the employee is on the right path.

Feedback through informal reviews and assessments

The onboarding period can take ninety days to a year, depending on the complexities of the new position and the needs of the employee. It is essential to conduct regular check-ins, ask how the employee is enjoying their work, and if anything can be done to improve or enhance their transition into the company. Missing this opportunity to assess the employee's productivity can lead to dissatisfaction in the long run.

25

Company culture immersion; get everyone on-board

During the onboarding period, a new employee is likely to connect your written policies with what they see demonstrated by others. Dress code, work hours, work style of colleagues and interactions of top-down leadership are all part of company culture. Ensure that what you state to be true in written policy form is truly representative in practice. And then your new employee will be "on board" the same train with the rest of your staff.

Making Orientation Something Fun and Engaging

26

Great orientations require the right facilitator.

The orientation leader should effectively represent the company culture, values and mission, and be comfortable delivering the material with enthusiasm and consistency. They should present a checklist of subjects that have been approved by management.

Establish a training plan that works.

Training sessions may include classroom-style training, on-the-job training, or a combination of both. Ensure all individuals involved in training understand their assigned subjects and stay on track. A solid training outline ensures there is no confusion over what topics should be covered. Clearly outline the required expectations and learning outcomes to ensure the new employee receives the information they need.

28

Develop content using adult learning styles.

An orientation program is as much about the company as it is about the new employee. Whether it's a brief overview, a one-day session or a week-long program, it should be developed in a manner that is focused on the learner. That includes utilizing effective adult-learning training techniques to deliver the important orientation training, such as learner-led activities and games to conquer boring lecture-style training.

Mix up the type of training.

Consider a training curriculum that effectively incorporates various adult learning styles, including visual, auditory, and kinesthetic. Adults bring with them past knowledge and experience that should be taken into account in the training process. Make sure the trainer is comfortable with designing and delivering material for all learning styles. If not, consider hiring outside curriculum developers to meet all needs.

30

Don't assume they will read it.

Providing a handbook and company policy manual is important during the onboarding period, but just handing out a copy to a new employee isn't enough. It behooves you to create a fun and interactive approach to sharing the information, such as creating a fun game or scavenger hunt that requires a deep dive into the material and allows them to gain insight on what's important and what you want them to know.

Covering the dry legal mumbo jumbo

It's okay, and actually preferable, to look for ways to make the legal information interesting and riveting for a new employee. Think of Southwest Airlines and the humor they are known for in covering safety information. Using real-life examples, asking questions, and injecting humor into mandatory material will make it more appealing and increase the likelihood of retention. An engaged audience is a satisfied audience.

32

Topics, procedures, and safety, oh my!

Covering safety is crucial in every new-hire orientation process. Even if you aren't in a regulated industry, including topics such as fire exits, evacuation protocol, accident and injury reporting procedures, OSHA standards and Whistleblower policies are important. It's also a great time to obtain input from new employees on their safety ideas and suggestions. An engaged and informed employee is a safe employee.

33

Stick to the agenda; avoid sidetracking.

Questions in new hire orientation are great--but too many sidebars can lead the facilitator off topic. Stay on track by responding to short questions and tabling lengthy or individualized discussions for later. Or provide an opportunity for the participant to contact you directly afterward to get their questions answered. Use a whiteboard or notepad to keep track of open questions.

Thinking Past Old Employee Benefit Plans

34

What are the benefits of benefits?

A strong employee benefit package not only "benefits" the employee, but also has long-term rewards for the employer. A competitive benefits package can be an effective recruiting and retention tool, helping to attract and retain great talent. Keep in mind that some benefits will have positive impact on costs, such as Flexible Spending Account (FSA), where tax-free payroll deductions can reduce employee and employer matching taxes.

35

What costs and what pays off

Search out win/win alternatives and the types of benefits employees want. Medical, Dental, Vision, Vacation/PTO are generally the most in demand. Do your research and analyze the best plans, using a broker if necessary. You don't have to lead your industry in benefits, but you want to stay competitive in the options you provide. Conduct an analysis every year to ensure you aren't missing new and important changes.

36

Benefits require decisions to be made.

When it comes to health insurance and wellness benefits, there are many options from which to choose. Research your competitors to find out what they may offer and look into offering comparable benefit plans. Consider hiring a smart insurance broker who can save you time and money by conducting hours of research. Allow them to lend their know-how to assist you in making the best decision for your business.

37

Be a super savvy benefits consumer.

One size does not fit all when selecting a competitive benefits plan. Consider surveying your current employees before making decisions on plans. Inquire into what does and doesn't appeal to them about their current benefits and other offers they'd like to see. Many employers offer benefits or insurance coverage that the employees don't value. Avoid wasting your money on something they don't use and remain open to change.

38

Don't give away the farm unnecessarily.

Employees want to know that their basic needs are covered; in other words, peace of mind. You may offer a long list of benefits, but if they aren't utilized, or if your pay, rewards or recognition programs aren't competitive, you may find it difficult to attract or retain employees. Find out what is wanted, what fits within your company culture and budget, and provide what is important to your employees.

39

How to offer
more for less

Sometimes, it's the small inexpensive things that are priceless and have meaning to employees. Consider an employee appreciation committee that plans events and gives input. Schedule regular lunches, movie days, birthday celebrations or parties where employees can interact in less formal settings. These can be low-cost, but provide opportunities to improve company culture and group cohesiveness.

40

Out of the box, intangible benefits

Today's employees value time, community and schedule flexibility. Find ways to tap into creative rewards. Can you offer telecommuting or flexible work schedules? Can you grant unscheduled early outs on Friday afternoons? Do you allow time off for volunteer activities or donations to an employee's favorite charity? Employees appreciate your attempt to understand their priorities.

Simplify the benefits to make sense.

Streamline the details of your company benefit package. Provide a one-page summary with brief explanations and important names, contact information and websites. Create a central location on your company intranet or server to store detailed information and summaries, such as the Summary Plan Description (SPD) and Summary of Benefits Coverage (SBC) for easy employee access. Stay in compliance with federal and state laws.

42

Ask for benefits feedback with survey.

Conduct an annual benefits survey to help you assess what is important to keep or modify when reviewing health insurance quotes. Additionally, employees may provide information about what will provide job satisfaction. An example might be they want higher deductible plans for lower premiums. You don't know until you ask and it's important to consider their best interests, as well as the bottom line.

Making the Effort to Manage Employees

43

Communication in theory and practice

Regular top-down communication with employees is vital in keeping employees engaged and on track. Starting at the highest levels, leadership should regularly send out progress updates on the company standings and financials. Share success stories through emails, newsletters or all-employee meetings. Employees want to hear from you. Create a mechanism for gathering their feedback. Be open to new ideas from all levels.

44

Establish employee engagement and recognition programs.

Work hard, play hard is a motto for a reason. Whether you have a large budget or very little to tap into, there are a plethora of ways to recognize your employees. Set team and department goals and when they are met, celebrate with a party. Implement employee-nominated recognition and hold annual recognition events. It doesn't take much to ensure you're recognizing the best of the best.

45

When an employee files a complaint

Employees must be provided a safe environment where they feel comfortable submitting concerns and/or complaints. Whether it's a satisfaction complaint or a potential harassment or discrimination claim, you want them to come to you. Always take the complaint seriously, let them know you will investigate, remain discreet and promptly address the issue-- no matter how small. Failure to do so will lead to lack of confidence in management.

46

Keep calm when discussing sensitive matters.

It's not easy dealing with an employee who is emotionally distraught or upset. Keep yourself in control by being clear, staying calm, and avoid getting caught up in their emotions. State objective facts rather than emotional data. Allow the employee to provide their input and feedback without interruption. Be aware of your tone of voice, hand gestures and body language that may come across as overly aggressive.

47

Interoffice drama; who's stirring the pot?

Be in tune with your employees and quick to squash office drama, gossip or pot-stirring. These issues create a negative work environment. Identify the employee creating issues and address their actions with no tolerance for their negative behavior. Obtain and document all the facts before taking corrective action. If you don't shut down the behavior, your work environment will deteriorate rapidly and morale will decline.

No employee is above the rules.

It doesn't matter how talented an employee is or how much revenue they generate, or what their position is, if their behavior poses a liability to your company, address the issues quickly and consistently. You should never tolerate bad behavior from anyone, regardless of position. Allowing immoral, illegal or unethical behavior to continue may cost you in legal expenses and loss of good employees because of it.

49

How to deal with *that* employee

It is important to identify how an employee is affecting morale, teamwork, and productivity. Don't blow off reports you receive about employee behaviors. Acknowledge them and follow through by addressing the issues. Make sure to document information concerning the employee with manager notes, coaching, and in-person interactions. Provide facts on how their behavior impacts the work environment and give them opportunity to improve the situation.

50

When it becomes 90210 at work

Social bullying is a reality in many offices. While it's important for employees to develop strong working relationships, some social cliques or relationships can negatively impact performance if they exclude or alienate others, intentionally or unintentionally. They may even cross the line into harassment or discrimination. Identify signs of these behaviors as soon as possible and take action to address them before they become bigger issues.

51

Dealing with
she said, they said

Disagreements exist in the workplace, and sometimes you must step in to mediate. Keep an open mind when this occurs so you can help objectively resolve differences. Ultimately, you may need to rely on your gut, and it may come down to the person with the most compelling or believable story. If there is not enough evidence to support either side, resolution may be agreeing to disagree and moving on.

Learning to get along with everyone

There is no rule that you must like everyone you work with, but as the employer, you must demand respect for each employee. When differences arise, highlight the positives and where they do agree, and build from there. Use and employ the Golden Rule, treating each other with professionalism and acting with integrity. If an employee doesn't adhere to this, then they must reconsider their interest in working in that environment.

53

The key to good employee relations

Trust your employee to do their job. Once you've hired and trained the right people, let them do it without micromanaging their work. Trust but verify. Delegate and spot check as needed and follow up regularly, but don't micromanage your employees. If there are problems that arise with behavior or performance, address them immediately.

54

Maintain healthy boundaries with your employees.

Developing rapport and healthy relationships with your employees is essential for employee engagement, but be careful of crossing a line or overstepping boundaries. This can be a downfall when employers get too involved with employees' personal business. Provide outlets for personal discussions with an Employee Assistance Program (EAP) or a Human Resources representative if you do not have one on staff.

55

Never make assumptions, verify your information.

Don't build stories in your head about someone's unusual behavior. For instance, if someone is acting differently or unusually irrational, it doesn't necessarily mean there is a drug or mental health issue. There could be many reasons for their uncharacteristic behavior. Do, however, address how the observed behavior affects performance. Ask them what they need from you and consider professional help, if necessary.

Batter up: assessing your organizational line-up

Identify your key positions and players and your organization's future. If you don't have a strategic plan in place, or don't know where you want to go, you will never get there. The same holds for talent. Determine where you want to be, create goals and then assess what talent you have ready to go now and identify your bench players who can be trained and groomed.

57

When they aren't ready for promotion

There may be times when an employee believes they are ready for a promotion, but you have a different opinion. At that point an honest conversation has to happen regarding their interests, skills and areas of development. If their skill level is not where it should be, work with them to develop an Individual Development Plan (IDP) outlining specific metrics or skills to acquire, in preparation for future promotional opportunities.

58

Use Emotional Intelligence for employee relations.

Learning how to harness the value of Emotional Intelligence (EI) is a powerful skill and one that studies have shown is the number one predictor of a leader's long-term success. Emotional Intelligence is the awareness of self, social awareness and the ability to read and recognize what others are feeling. A leader who can adapt to social norms is far greater at diffusing conflict and therefore building better employee relations.

Performance Isn't Just an Annual Discussion

59

Workforce trends drive talent management strategies.

Identify critical positions that are core and necessary to meeting your operational goals. Consider your customer base and whether your workforce is representative of that population. Create a workforce plan to ensure that you have the right talent, when you need it and that the talent is trained with the proper skillsets. Be cognizant of workforce trends.

60

Feedback isn't just for annual reviews.

An annual review is a culmination of an employee's work performance, a time to look to the future and to set goals. However, the review shouldn't be saved for a one-and-done review. Feedback should be an ongoing process. Regular check-ins should be held throughout the year to provide consistent feedback on performance. When it comes to an employee's annual review, nothing should come as a surprise to them.

61

Create a culture of promoting within.

Look to develop in-house talent before hiring externally for an open position. Evaluate your current workforce and post vacant positions internally first, to allow for development of your existing staff. Hold annual talent reviews to evaluate the skills and knowledge base of your current workforce. If they don't pair up, create and identify growth assignments for individuals and be prepared to offer solid feedback for improvement.

62

Identify employee capabilities, skills and strengths.

To keep valuable employees, engage them through development assignments and opportunities. This can be done through assessments, discussions, performance observations, and work product feedback. Don't be afraid to ask the employee the question, "What do you want to do?" and follow it up with a plan to help them achieve those goals. Failure to do this may lead to employee disengagement and potential loss of good employees.

63

Match employee talent with company vision.

Once you've identified your organizational strategy, and evaluated employee skills, the next step is aligning those goals with talents and career aspirations. Spend time mapping out the employee's career trajectory within your organization. Will you need more managers? Is there new technology they may be able to support in the future? Let them know how valuable they will be to the future success of the company.

Capitalize on diversity in your workforce.

Cookie cutter workplaces rarely lend themselves well to gaining the competitive advantage in the marketplace. If you want your business to thrive, hiring and promoting talented and diverse employees is critical to thriving in today's world. Look for individuals who not only have the skills, but may offer differing opinions, experiences and ideas to increase your business's foothold in the market.

65

Create an effective employee performance evaluation.

Employees need feedback to continue to meet your expectations. The annual review process is feedback-focused on achievements and future expectations. Evaluation should include objective feedback on highlighted achievements and future goals in conjunction with the employee's insights. Administer a system using SMARTER goals (**S**pecific, **M**easurable, **A**ttainable, **R**elevant, **T**ime-bound, **E**valuate, **R**e-evaluate).

66

Feedback should be regular and constructive.

Keeping an employee engaged ensures they are challenged in their work, which means providing appropriate stretch goals and giving timely and regular feedback. This requires regular check-ins to update progress on goals, improvement areas or development plans. Employees don't know how they are performing if they don't hear from you. Schedule time on a regular basis to provide consistent feedback on how you think they are performing.

67

Performance evaluations are living breathing documents.

Although you may only meet annually to conduct performance reviews, discussions should be taking place on a regular basis. Even quick check-ins done quarterly are enough to ensure the employee is on track for meeting their time-bound goals. This keeps both you and the employee accountable to their work product. The employee should take ownership on goals, but the manager should take charge of it.

Great performers with poor interpersonal skills

Some employees have the skills to out-perform others, but horrible interpersonal skills. These people constantly over-achieve, but at a cost that can often sacrifice teamwork and morale. They should be evaluated on both "what" they do and "how" they do it. If they mistreat others, disrespect their colleagues or employ bullying methods as a means to an end, they must learn that you will not tolerate that behavior.

69

Provide balanced and effective performance feedback.

An employee needs to hear specific, constructive and balanced feedback on their overall achievement. As the manager, it's important to evaluate the entire performance period, providing both quantitative and qualitative feedback. Review their overall achievements--what you observed, heard or witnessed--and how their work impacted the bottom line. The more details and data, the better.

70

Correct poor performance before annual reviews.

You must be honest with performance assessments throughout the year before it becomes a problem. Monthly or quarterly check-ins are useful in redirecting missteps and coaching the employee, circumventing any issues. Highlight areas of concern, explain the impact their performance has on the team, customer or business, and collaborate on a resolution or plan to improve. The annual review is not the time to bring up a new issue.

71

It's not a birthday. No surprises.

Surprises are best left to celebrations, not annual reviews. An employee should never receive feedback for the first time during their review. Regular check-ins and coaching sessions are imperative. When the manager coaches regularly, ensure it's documented with written confirmations. An email noting the conversation will ensure that when review time comes, the feedback is not coming out of left field.

Seeking HR support before disaster strikes

If a manager thinks an upcoming review may prove difficult, they should seek out HR support to prepare for effective message delivery. This may include discussions between manager and HR to lay out the discussion plan, tips on how to best communicate with the employee, and how to remain on track during the review. HR may also serve as editor to review the final written comments before delivery.

73

Consistently document and address employee performance.

Documenting performance memorializes the conversation, identifies when it took place, what was discussed, and the commitments made. Failure to document may leave a manager with a faulty recollection. And if no progress is made, it can help in future disciplinary actions. Consistently document not only errors, but achievements and improvement.

Keeping the Difficult Out of Conversations

74

Not everything smells like a rose.

Speaking with an employee about body odor or scent can be difficult. However, it may be necessary if another employee has brought it forward. Many fragrances and strongly scented perfumes can make people sick and wreak havoc on their immune systems. Choose your words wisely so as not to make the person feel unnecessarily uncomfortable or embarrassed. State the facts and avoid blame or insult.

75

What about the donkeys and elephants?

Few people can respectfully agree to disagree when it comes to politics. In the workplace, however, do not make employment-related decisions based solely on political views. While political ideology is not a protected class under the federal law, it may be at state and local levels. Extreme disagreements could lead to discrimination and/or discord. You may need to step into the conversation to keep things neutral.

76

Standing up to the office bully.

Bullying in and of itself is not illegal or punishable by law, but if it goes beyond words to threats, physical violence, discrimination or stalking, then it may be. Learn to recognize signs of bullying behavior and address complaints from employees or employee feedback forums. Some employees use loud tones or strong words to make themselves heard. Provide consistent and unbiased feedback on how they are perceived.

Drawing the line on insubordinate employees.

Employees should be encouraged to voice their opinions, but in the appropriate manner and at the right time and place. Respectful disagreement is acceptable as long as the employee understands the manager has final decision-making authority. Provide employees opportunities and methods to share concerns. However, once a management decision is made, policies must be followed. Insubordination should not be tolerated.

78

Watercooler talk can negatively impact morale.

While it is important to maintain an open-door policy for employees to express their concerns, many choose to discuss issues amongst themselves. This may have both positive and negative impacts on the organization. Gossips and complainers breed discontentment and lower morale and productivity. Encourage open dialogue through staff meetings with management.

79

Dishonesty: liars, cheaters, thieves and morale.

Dishonest or unethical behavior in the workplace is a symptom of something deeper and can hurt the organization. Not having an internal whistle-blowing policy or avoiding the issues can condone the behavior. It is important to have a policy in your company handbook to encourage ethical, moral behavior and for employees to have a way to report the behavior anonymously.

80

How to deal with traumatic events

Regardless of your industry or the safety hazards in your business, you should have a procedure to follow in the event of a traumatic event, such as an accident or fatality. Establish protocol for reporting accidents and for employees to request help, if needed. Be prepared for the unexpected and ensure your employees know what to do. As best practices, have a Safety Plan and Emergency Preparedness in place.

Less is more in the workplace.

There's a fine line between establishing trust and crossing the line into friend territory. As a manager, you must know where the relationship boundaries exist when you are in a leadership position. Be careful when indulging in extracurricular activities, social media, and social functions. Have an open-door policy, but avoid oversharing your own personal views, experiences or problems with the employee. Stay neutral, yet empathetic.

82

Nobody said management would be easy.

Difficult conversations with employees can be uncomfortable but are necessary in setting expectations, improving performance, or mitigating problems in the office. Prepare for the conversation by ensuring there is enough time and privacy. Establish bullet points for discussion topics, outlining issues, impacts and employee actions. Ask for feedback on the resolution and clarification if needed.

New Ways to Make Training Stick

83

Don't expect what you haven't taught.

You may have hired great talent, but don't assume the employee has the exact knowledge, skills and abilities needed if you haven't developed them. Perhaps they had a wealth of experience using a CRM or an accounting tool, but it may differ from your processes or systems. You must assess and identify gaps in understanding, then implement strategies to coach and train the employee to meet your expectations.

Teach soft skills to promote harmony.

Not every employee is equipped with perfectly polished interpersonal skills. Even the brightest and best may have difficulty working well with others. However, don't allow the lack of soft skills to be a mainstay. Provide direct and consistent feedback using your observations of the employee, and clearly set the tone and expectations for what you want to see. No person is an island, and strong interpersonal skills are a must.

85

How to develop a training program

Don't jump to conclusions about whether training is needed. First, decide whether it is a training issue or a systemic process issue by using the ADDIE model (Analysis, Design, Development, Implementation, and Evaluation.) Identifying if there is a performance gap is step one. Gather data to determine the type of issue. If it's a training issue, identify objectives, evaluate options, estimate budget and determine a timeline.

86

Technical training is a must have.

The pace of technology is speedier than ever and constantly changing on a dime, so it's up to the company to provide the necessary training to keep up and ahead of the competition. But before jumping on every new bandwagon, make sure you've balanced the benefit with the cost of staying ahead of the curve. It may be the newest, greatest tool, but what will be your return on investment?

87

On the job training is essential.

Managers must devote time to the training process, providing on-the-job training in the work environment. Providing hands-on training will get your new employee up to speed faster and with greater success. This training can be facilitated by the manager or by a competent senior employee you have selected. Ensure that a training checklist is utilized and you are kept apprised of the learning process through regular check-ins.

88

Cassettes versus MP3s; generations are different.

Generational differences should influence training. While learning styles are universal, there are generational distinctions. Some may be interested in informal, highly personal, self-directed training; while others favor self-directed options and are fiercely independent. Others require transformational and informational learning. Use blended options including on-demand, flexible and one-on-one approaches in your programs.

89

Annual training reinforces the best practices.

Depending on your industry, there may be required certification courses or compliance training. Establish a master spreadsheet or database of courses your employees need and when you offered them, tracking their participation. Offering regulatory or compliance training annually limits liability, lawsuits and/or fines. Seek out a professional training practitioner or HR consultant for custom or off-the-shelf courses.

90

Lean on me: rely on HR.

Even managers need guidance and help sometimes to determine required versus recommended training. Calling upon an HR trainer, who has the specialized skills, knowledge and expertise to facilitate the training, will alleviate the burden from managers who try to take on this time-consuming process. While training might look easy, there are many components that go into creating and leading effective adult learning sessions.

91

Training retreats build a strong team.

There are times when the best approach to building cohesive teams is to get out of the office. Hosting a team retreat can be critical in strengthening unity amongst your employees. When there is a common goal or project at stake, retreats build rapport, strengthen bonds, and help to identify and eliminate team dysfunctions. It may also provide opportunities to create mission statements and long-term team goals.

92

Training adults: understand how they learn.

Adult learners bring experience to the workplace and must know why they are learning something and how it applies to the job. To enhance the value of learning, identify their motivations and interests. Understand and implement the three adult-learning styles and training methods: visual, kinesthetic and auditory. Allow them to implement what they learned immediately.

The Next Generation Needs Your Coaching

93

Succession planning: future days, future leaders.

Succession planning should be a high priority for all businesses. It identifies high-potential employees to fill future key leadership roles. Planning should occur annually with these categories: potential for next promotion, diversity, abilities and aspirations, as well as coaching and training opportunities. This is a time-consuming activity, but will give your organization leadership security and align employee ambitions with key roles.

94

Develop your leaders through ID Plans.

Great leaders aren't just born; they are developed. When building strong leaders, both classroom training and coaching sessions may be used. Implementing a human resource intervention, such as a formalized coaching plan, Individual Development Plan (IDP) and a Competency Map, will keep you and your employee accountable to their development.

95

Evolving individual development plans for growth

An IDP should become a living, breathing document. Just as the business changes, so should thc IDP opportunities. Revisit it with your employee on a regular basis, at the very least, every six months. Update the available opportunities and identify where they want to be. Neither you nor the employee should be worried about changing directions, if that's what it takes to get to the right result.

96

Promote the skills not the longevity.

Many managers often make the mistake of promoting an employee who demonstrates technical knowledge or has seniority, but may not demonstrate the interpersonal skills required for a leadership role. Important factors to consider are not only their technical skills, but do they possess a strong leadership style? If they are promoted, do they have the ambition and desire to do the job? Simple assessments can be used to determine these attributes.

97

Rotational roles can steadily increase competency.

Challenging emerging leaders with unfamiliar roles stretches their competency levels. For example, if you are developing an operational leader, they should spend time in each department, such as finance, marketing and business development. Schedule rotational job changes every six months to a year to allow the leader to become immersed and experienced in each role. Provide feedback along the way for maximum growth.

98

How to develop an "A" player.

Developing top performers takes more than just a promotion. To get that next generational leader ready for the next role, invest time in their talent. For example, even a highly ranked rookie baseball player is trained before their first pro game. Spend time assessing their areas of opportunity and then coaching to those weaknesses. Educate them, increase their work scope, and increase their breadth of responsibility before promoting.

99

Create mentoring programs with senior managers.

Mentor programs can range from simple to complex based on your organizational needs. The key is to enable current leaders to pass on their institutional knowledge and know-how to help future leaders. Examples may include rotating lunch schedules to discuss a variety of topics, mentoring a new project from start to finish, or creating a checklist of milestones for the emerging leader to complete.

100

Let your employees become your teachers.

Give employees opportunities through various forums to instruct others in their jobs or organizational matters. A lunchtime learning session brings employees together and helps the organization capitalize on the talents of their employee base to share expertise. For example, you may have an employee who is a whiz at Excel; allow them to give an overview to other employees.

Note from the Author

Thank you for reading our book. I hope that you found some useful information to apply to your work with your employees. We would love to hear your thoughts.

For feedback or additional information about our services or speaking engagements, please visit our website at JBConsultingSystems.com and click on "Contact Us."

About the Six-Word Lessons Series

Legend has it that Ernest Hemingway was challenged to write a story using only six words. He responded with the story, "For sale: baby shoes, never worn." The story tickles the imagination. Why were the shoes never worn? The answers are left up to the reader's imagination.

This style of writing has a number of aliases: postcard fiction, flash fiction, and micro fiction. Lonnie Pacelli was introduced to this concept in 2009 by a friend, and started thinking about how this extreme brevity could apply to today's communication culture of text messages, tweets and Facebook posts. He wrote the first book, *Six-Word Lessons for Project Managers*, then he and his wife Patty started helping other authors write and publish their own books in the series.

The books all have six-word chapters with six-word lesson titles, each followed by a one-page description. They can be written by entrepreneurs who want to promote their businesses, or anyone with a message to share.

See the entire ***Six-Word Lessons Series*** at **6wordlessons.com**

Made in the USA
Columbia, SC
21 July 2021